Contents

Some words in the book are in bold, **like this**. You can find out what they mean by looking in the glossary.

Introducing Hungary

What do you know about Hungary? Maybe you have eaten Hungarian goulash. But do you know about Hungary's history, how its people spend their time, or what the country looks like?

A unique nation

Hungary is a country in central Europe with a fascinating and tragic history, and a colourful folk **culture**. It covers an area of 93,028 square kilometres (35,918 square miles), which is slightly smaller than Scotland and Wales put together. Hungary's countryside includes rolling plains and hills, and beautiful rivers and lakes. Hungarians are proud of their country and their national character has been affected by their war-torn past.

Changing times

Over the centuries, there have been many disputes about which lands belong to the Hungarians, and the lands have been **occupied** by foreign powers. The Hungary we recognize today has only existed as a nation since 1920. In more recent years, Hungary has become a popular tourist destination and life in the country has changed dramatically.

Read on to find out what makes Hungary and its people so unusual and interesting.

How to say...

Hi! *Szia* (SI-o)
Hello *Szervusz* (SER-vus)
How are you? *Hogy van?* (hawd von)
Goodbye *Viszontlátásra* (VI-sawnt-laa-taash-ro)
Yes *Igen* (I-gen)
No *Nem* (nem)
Please *Kérem* (KAY-rem)
Thank you *Köszönöm* (KEU-seu-neum)
Young Hungarians say "hello" as a slang way of saying goodbye!

The river Danube flows through the middle of Budapest, Hungary's capital city.

History: invasions and independence

There have been people living in the Hungarian lands for at least half a million years. Around 2000 BC, **tribes** from the Balkans settled there and by the early 300s BC Celts were living in Hungary. The Romans ruled from 35 BC, as they did in most of Europe. They gradually took over more and more land in the region and introduced building technology, writing, and winemaking.

Roman rule ended when Huns invaded from the east. Then, other tribes from German lands, such as the Goths, Avars, and Franks, came to the region. The great Frankish king Charlemagne brought **Christianity** to the people there.

Magyars

The Magyar people were **nomadic** tribes who settled in the Hungarian lands during the middle of the AD 800s. The Magyar ruler Árpád is said to have united the Magyars. Then, on 25 December 1000, the Magyar Prince Stephen was crowned king and the nation of Hungary was founded. Today, the Republic of Hungary is called *Magyar Köztársaság* in Hungarian.

However, this unity was short-lived and from 1038 to 1301 there were power struggles within Hungary. Neighbouring rulers saw this as a chance to take land from the Hungarians, and the kingdom was weakened once more.

KING STEPHEN I [C. 967-1038]

King Stephen I was the first king of Hungary, reigning from 1000 to 1038. King Stephen made Christianity the dominant religion in the kingdom of Hungary and **occupied** new lands. He had good judgement in making **alliances** that kept his kingdom strong and united. He was made a saint after his death.

This statue of King Stephen I stands in Budapest.

The Turks and the Habsburgs

King Louis I (1326–1382), known as Louis the Great, made Hungary powerful again. But the Ottoman Turks were a new threat. The Turkish army defeated the teenage King Louis II at the Battle of Mohács in 1526.

The Turks occupied central Hungary until the 1600s. Western Hungary was controlled by the Habsburgs, a powerful royal family with an empire across much of Europe. Transylvania ruled the east of Hungary. When the Turks left, Hungarians faced wars with European powers for many years.

Suleiman the Magnificent was the Turkish sultan who defeated Hungary in 1526.

War and chaos

From 1848 to 1849, the Hungarians fought a War of Independence but were defeated by the Habsburg Emperor Franz Joseph. Many Hungarians were executed and the country was merged into the Habsburg Empire again. However, in 1867, the struggle for independence was partly won when the Austro-Hungarian Empire was formed, with capitals in Vienna in Austria and Pest in Hungary. Hungary's **economy** and **culture** flourished, but working-class people still struggled to make a living.

World War I began in 1914 and Hungary fought alongside Germany. Hundreds of thousands of Hungarians died.

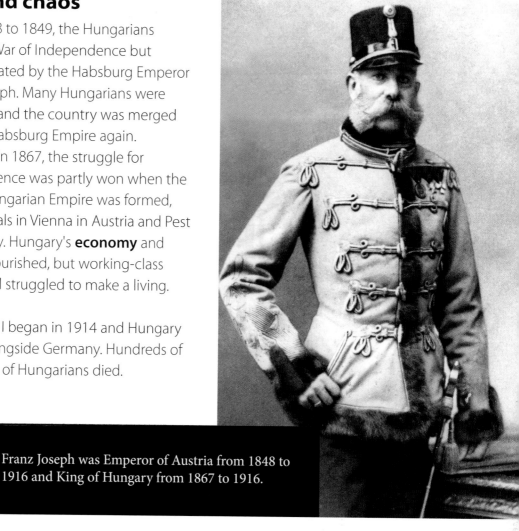

Franz Joseph was Emperor of Austria from 1848 to 1916 and King of Hungary from 1867 to 1916.

Daily life

In the second half of the 1800s, Hungary became more **industrialized**. The middle classes grew in the cities and most of the country's working classes lived in the capital, Budapest. These workers could not vote, and were paid very low wages. In the countryside, peasants lived as they had for thousands of years. As the population grew there was less land to share and farmers could barely make a living.

World War II

At the start of World War II, Hungary was on the same side as Germany and Italy. Thousands of Hungarians died fighting the **Soviet Union**. The Hungarian leader, Horthy, began talking to the **Allies** but **Nazi** Germany's leader, Adolf Hitler, reacted by setting up a pro-Nazi government in Hungary. The country's **Jewish** population was put into **ghettos** and 70 per cent of Hungarian Jews were killed in **concentration camps**, such as Auschwitz.

Much of Budapest was destroyed in the fighting during World War II.

Communist Hungary

After the war, Hungary became a **democracy** but eventually the **communists** took control. The country was industrialized and farmers' land was taken and made into collective farms. Many people were arrested and jailed. In 1956, there was an uprising and students demonstrated, pulling down a statue of the Soviet leader, Stalin. Imre Nagy became prime minister. He talked about **reform**, and released political prisoners. Then, Nagy announced that Hungary would no longer be allied to the Soviet Union. The Soviet Union reacted by sending in troops and tanks. Fighting went on for days and 25,000 people were killed.

This map shows which countries in Europe became communist after World War II.

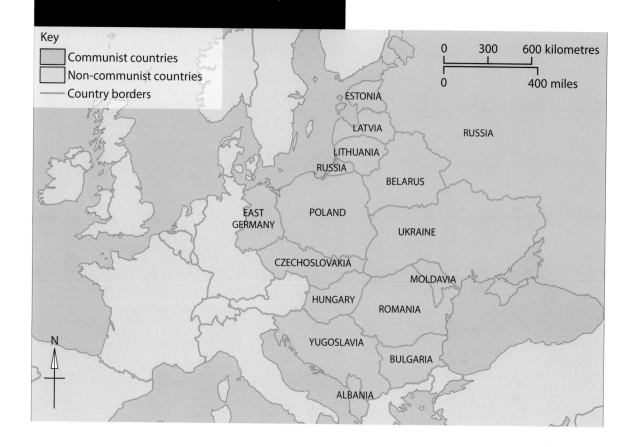

Key
- Communist countries
- Non-communist countries
- Country borders

0   300   600 kilometres

0   400 miles

ESTONIA

LATVIA

LITHUANIA

RUSSIA

RUSSIA

BELARUS

EAST GERMANY

POLAND

UKRAINE

CZECHOSLOVAKIA

MOLDAVIA

HUNGARY

ROMANIA

YUGOSLAVIA

BULGARIA

ALBANIA

N

IMRE NAGY [1896–1958]

Imre Nagy was born into a peasant family and fought in World War I. He was prime minister of Hungary from 1953 to 1955, but was sacked when he didn't do what the Soviets wanted. He became prime minister again in 1956 but was soon arrested. He was executed by the Soviets in 1958.

When the border fence with Austria came down, many people took the opportunity to move to the West.

End of communism

The communists realized change was needed. The government became quite **liberal** and people had more freedom than in countries such as Czechoslovakia and East Germany. This was known as "goulash socialism" because it was uniquely Hungarian, like the famous dish.

People from all backgrounds enjoyed a good standard of living. But during the 1980s, unemployment and debt caused problems. It was hard for people to travel to the **West**, but in 1989 Hungarians began to take down the electric fence on the Austrian border. Suddenly, many Hungarians and East Germans travelled into the West and changes began to take place across central and eastern Europe.

YOUNG PEOPLE

Zsuzsanna Clark is a Hungarian writer who grew up in the 1970s and 80s. She remembers a crime-free society with good education and healthcare. There was a sense of friendship and trust and everyone could enjoy holidays and outings. Zsuzsanna especially enjoyed being a member of the Pioneers, a group similar to the Scouts. Pioneers had strong friendships and worked together to help the community.

The new Hungary

In 1990, free elections were held in Hungary and it became the Republic of Hungary. The government no longer controlled businesses and farms and the economy was opened up. In 2004, Hungary joined the European Union (**EU**) and Hungarians were free to live and work in other EU countries.

Not all the changes have been good. Crime has risen, and many people struggle to find work and cope with rising prices. Large demonstrations against the government took place in 2006. The global economic crisis, which began in 2008, has caused further problems.

Regions and resources: land of lakes and plains

Hungary is **landlocked** and has borders with seven other countries. Austria is to the north-west, with Slovakia to the north. Ukraine and Romania lie to Hungary's east, while Serbia and Croatia are on its southern border. Slovenia borders Hungary in the west. Hungary's capital city is Budapest, which lies just north of the centre of the country.

The Hungarian landscape is mostly flat plains, with some hills and low mountains on the border with Slovakia. The country's climate is made up of cold winters and warm summers. Average summer temperatures are around 27°C (80°F), while winter temperatures range from -1 to -4°C (30.2 to 24.8°F). Rainfall is heaviest in May and November.

Land height
- Over 1000 metres
- Over 400 metres
- Over 200 metres
- Above sea level
- Country borders

This map shows that much of Hungary is low-lying land.

Many people enjoy the waters of Lake Balaton during the summer.

Landscape and features

Hungary's plains dominate its landscape, with 80 per cent of the land lying below 200 metres (656 feet). Fifty per cent of this land is used for agriculture. The highest mountain is Kékes, standing at 1,014 metres (3,326 feet) high. The second longest river in Europe, the Danube (Duna), flows through Hungary. Another large river is the Tisza. Lake Balaton in the west is the largest freshwater lake in Europe, covering 596 square kilometres (230 square miles). Lake Gyógy-tó in the same region is the largest **thermal** lake in Europe.

How to say...

cave *barlang* (BAR-laung)
forest *erdö* (ER-deu)
hill *domb* (Dom-B)
island *sziget* (SI-get)
lake *tó* (taw)
meadow *legelő* (LEG-eleu)
mountain *hegy* (hedge)
plain *alföld* (AL-feuld)
river *folyó* (FO-yo)

Around the Danube

The River Danube flows through Hungary from north to south. Along its banks is the capital city Budapest, which was created when the cities of Buda and Pest were joined. Buda lies on hilly land on the west bank of the river, while Pest is on a flat plain on the eastern side.

The hilly area west of Budapest is Central Transdanubia. Lake Velence and Lake Balaton are found here. Western Transdanubia in the north-west of the country has thermal springs, castles, rivers, lakes, and wetlands. Southern Transdanubia lies south of Lake Balaton and is mainly an agricultural region. Wine is produced in the warm climate there.

People swim in the warm water of Lake Gyógy-tó all year round.

Northern Hungary

In northern Hungary, there are mountains, forests, and caves. The caves of Aggtelek have incredible **geological** formations, with the largest group of stalactites in Europe. Traditional village life in the far north-east has changed very little for hundreds of years.

One of the caves at Aggtelek has such impressive stalactites, it has been made a World Heritage site.

The Great Plain

The Hungarian Great Plain lies in the south-east of the country. It covers 36,000 square kilometres (13,900 square miles) of flat land. Lake Tisza is in the central area of the plain, while in the east cattle are farmed on much of the land. The River Tisza flows through the Southern Great Plain, which is an important agricultural area.

Daily life

Life for **rural** people in Hungary is a mixture of traditional and modern. Many women still make folk **embroidery** and people enjoy folk dances. Rural homes are usually small cottages built in a traditional style. But most country people wear modern clothes and have access to modern technology. The growth of tourism across Hungary will modernize the rural areas even more.

The economy

Hungary's **economy** grew and developed well after 1990. Many foreign businesses invested in Hungary. But the economy has struggled since 2006 due to government debts and the global economic crisis that began in 2008. This has meant that **exports** have fallen and fewer goods are being sold within Hungary. In 2009, around 10.8 per cent of the working population was unemployed.

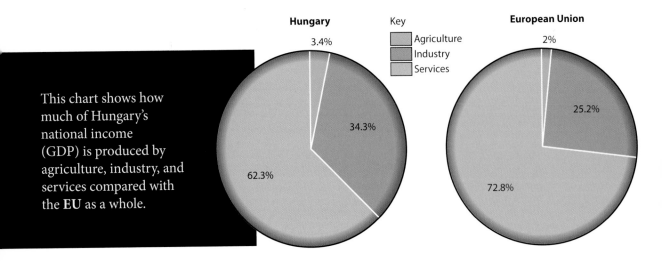

This chart shows how much of Hungary's national income (GDP) is produced by agriculture, industry, and services compared with the **EU** as a whole.

Hungary

3.4%

34.3%

62.3%

Key
- Agriculture
- Industry
- Services

European Union

2%

25.2%

72.8%

Industry and natural resources

Hungarian factories produce a range of goods. Some of the main industries include metal production, construction materials, processed foods, textiles, and chemicals. Many motor vehicles are manufactured in Hungary, mostly for foreign companies such as Audi, Opel, and Suzuki. The exports of these companies make up 17 per cent of all Hungarian exports.

Some important natural resources found in Hungary include bauxite (a mineral that contains aluminium), coal, and natural gas. Another key natural resource is fertile farming land. Hungarian farms produce wheat, corn, sunflower seeds, potatoes, and sugar beets. Farmers also rear pigs, cattle, and poultry, and produce dairy products.

This lignite (brown coal) mine is in the north-east of Hungary.

Key
△ Aluminium
▲ Zinc
△ Iron and steel
▲ Coal
△ Cement
△ Lead
△ Copper
▲ Uranium
⬤ Manganese
⬤ Natural gas
🝰 Petroleum
   refinery products

This map shows where important minerals can be found in Hungary.

Wildlife: protecting nature

There are 10 national parks in Hungary and over 1,400 conservation areas where animals and plants are protected. Hortobágy is the biggest national park and is found on the Great Plain in the east of the country. It is the largest natural grassland in Europe and is home to many important species of birds and plants. There is a special reserve there for the great bustard, which is the heaviest flying bird in the world.

Kiskunság National Park is also in the Great Plain and includes Lake Kolon, where marsh tortoises and nine species of orchid can be found. Danube-Drava National Park is in the south-west of the country and is home to over 400 protected plants and animals.

Hungarian wildlife

Some more common animals in Hungary are deer, hares, foxes, and wild boar. Rare animals include wolves, lynx, beavers, lake bats, and Pannonian lizards. There are many birds in Hungary, with a huge number of waterfowl living in the country's lakes and rivers. The rare black stork travels through Hungary, and great white egrets and white-tailed eagles can also be spotted.

There are around 2,200 plant species in Hungary, 535 of which are protected. These include the fragrant hellebore that grows in the Mecsek mountains, the wild peony, the sage of the Great Plain, and the meadow anemone. There are 47 native tree species in Hungary, six of which are **endangered**.

How to say...

bat *denevér* (DENE-vayr)
beaver *hód* (hawd)
bird *madár* (MA-daar)
deer *rőtvad* (REUT-vad)
fish *hal* (hawl)

lynx *hiúz* (HEE-oose)
squirrel *mókus* (MAW-koosh)
stork *gólya* (GAW-ya)
wolf *farkas* (FAR-kash)

The black stork visits
Hungary during the
warm summers.

Threatened species

Endangered animals in Hungary include the Danube crested newt, a type of salamander that lives in freshwater habitats in central Europe. Its numbers are threatened as its habitat is destroyed. The European ground squirrel has also lost much of its habitat due to agriculture and building.

Endangered birds include aquatic warblers, corncrakes, Egyptian vultures, Peregrine falcons, and great bustards. Protected areas have been set up to stop any further decline in the numbers of these species.

Various species of bat are under threat, such as this western barbastelle bat.

The environment

Since 2000, people in Hungary have become much more aware of environmental issues. Old coal-fired power stations made air pollution a problem for decades, but many of these stations have now been shut down, drastically reducing **emissions**. Cars that cause excessive pollution have been banned from Hungarian roads.

Some waterways are still polluted, mostly by farming chemicals. Membership of the **EU** means Hungary has to follow its regulations to prevent pollution. The Ministry of Environment and Water was also set up to change the damaging habits of the past.

These Hungarians are taking part in a cycle ride to encourage people to travel by bike to help the environment.

YOUNG PEOPLE

"Challenge Europe" is a project involving young Hungarians who are trying to make a difference to climate change. Sixteen young people are working to raise awareness in Hungary about carbon emissions and damage to the environment. Edina Barbara Budai is a student of **renewable energy** planning. She wants to work with children to pass on the message of environmental protection. Gergely Csima wants to be a sustainable farmer and encourage people to live in harmony with nature.

Infrastructure: head of state, homes, and hospitals

Since free elections were held in 1990, Hungary has been a parliamentary **democracy**. This type of government allows its people to vote for a president and representatives from a range of political parties. The president is the country's **head of state**, and holds the post for a five-year term. The head of government is the prime minister, who is elected by the National Assembly on the president's recommendation.

The prime minister leads a council of ministers that runs the government. The National Assembly is made up of 386 elected representatives. Hungary is a member of the North Atlantic Treaty Organization (**NATO**), the World Trade Organization (WTO), and the International Monetary Fund (IMF).

This map shows Hungary's 20 regional divisions.

Money

The **currency** in Hungary is the *forint* (Ft), which uses coins and banknotes. It was introduced in 1946. There are 1, 2, 5, 10, 20, 50, 100, and 200 Ft coins and 500, 1,000, 2,000, 5,000, 10,000, and 20,000 Ft banknotes. Hungary may move from the *forint* and use the **euro** in the future.

The pictures on Hungarian *forint* notes show many famous people from the country's history.

ISTVÁN SZÉCHENYI (1791–1860)

On the 5,000-*forint* note is a picture of István Széchenyi. Count Széchenyi was a writer and politician who wrote about how to improve the lives of peasants and **reform** the **economy**. He also did much for the country's **infrastructure**. He contributed towards the first bridge between Buda and Pest, Hungary's first railways, and the first steam transport on the country's lakes. He also donated money to the Academy of Science. Sadly, he suffered from mental illness towards the end of his life, but he is remembered for all his great contributions to Hungarian society.

School

In Hungary, three- to six-year-old children attend pre-school (called *óvoda*). They learn traditional poetry, songs, and music. Children start primary school at the age of 6, and finish at 14. They can then choose between an **academic** or **vocational** secondary school. The school day starts at about 8.00 a.m. and there are usually five or six 45-minute lessons in a day. The school year starts in September and ends in June. There are holidays at Christmas and at Easter.

Health

When Hungary was under **communist** rule, healthcare was free and generally of a high quality. However, treatments weren't always equally accessible across the country. Today, Hungary has a modern healthcare system but there are still problems. Hungarians lead active lives, but unhealthy activities, such as smoking and drinking too much alcohol, are still common. The World Health Organization (WHO) placed Hungary 66th out of 190 countries in its ranking of world health systems in 2000.

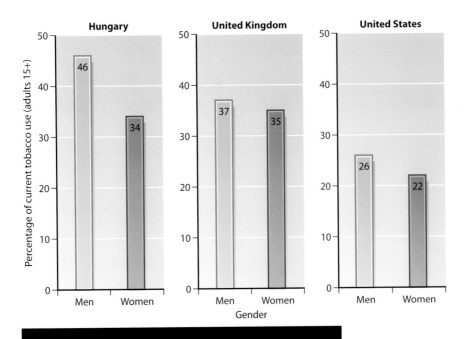

These bar charts compare how much tobacco is used in Hungary compared to the United Kingdom and the United States.

Daily life

Many people in Hungary's cities live in the **prefabricated** blocks of flats built by the old communist government. City people meet in cafés and during the summer there are outdoor entertainment gardens, called *kertek*, where parties are held. In Budapest another popular pastime is visiting the city's **thermal** baths, where people can relax in pools of different temperatures.

Culture: from folk traditions to goulash

Hungarians are very proud of their traditional folk **culture**. Hungarian folk music has spread in popularity throughout central Europe. **Roma** music is usually sung **a cappella**. But Hungarian culture goes beyond these folk traditions.

Daily life

The Roma people are a minority group who have lived in Hungary for centuries. They suffer discrimination and many live in poverty with a low life expectancy. Roma people are trying to keep their own language, music, and traditions alive. Other minority groups in Hungary include the **Jewish** and German-speaking populations.

Music

Hungary has produced world-famous **classical** composers, such as Ferenc Liszt, Zoltán Kodály, and Béla Bartók. Liszt set up the Academy of Music in Budapest, while Kodály and Bartók studied and recorded the country's folk music.

Rock music is also popular in Hungary. Home-grown groups include Illes, Metro, and Omega. There are several big music festivals, such as the Balaton Festival held by Lake Balaton in May, and the huge Sziget Festival held in Budapest during August.

These folk muscians are performing at a carnival in the southern city of Kaposvár.

Drama and dance

Hungarians enjoy theatre and cinema. Folk dance is performed at dance houses in Budapest and the Gyor Ballet's modern dance is famous around the world.

Although not many films are made in Hungary, they often win awards and praise. Directors such as Miklós Jancsó and István Szabó have become world-famous.

Art

Hungary has produced some great painters. Tivadar Csontváry-Kosztka (1853–1919) was an **Expressionist** artist who became a painter on hearing a voice telling him to do it! József Rippl-Rónai (1861–1927) created **Art Nouveau** paintings using bright colours and small brush strokes. Victor Vasarely (1908–97) created Op Art, a type of art that uses optical illusions.

Books

Some famous Hungarian writers include the poet Sandor Petofi (1823–49) and Zsigmond Moricz (1879–1942), who wrote about the hard lives of peasants in the 1800s. Because the Hungarian language is so unusual, not many works were translated or read in other countries. Under **communism** many writers were stopped from writing what they believed. Imre Kertesz is a Jewish writer who won the Nobel Prize for Literature in 2002. He survived the **Nazi** death camp at Auschwitz in World War II.

Magda Szabó is one of Hungary's most famous female writers.

FERENC KÖLCSEY (1790-1838)

Ferenc Kölcsey was a patriotic poet, critic, and politician. He wrote the poem *Himnusz* about Hungary's glorious past and this became the country's national anthem.

Sport

Hungary has won more Olympic medals per person than any other country. Hungarians tend to be good at water sports and enjoy watching football and water polo. The Hungarian Grand Prix takes place each summer near Budapest.

KRISZTINA EGERSZEGI [1974-]

The swimmer Krisztina Egerszegi was the youngest Olympic champion of her time. When she was 14, she won gold and silver medals at the 1988 Seoul Olympics. At the 1992 Barcelona Olympics she won three gold medals and at 1996 in Atlanta she won a gold and bronze medal.

The Spanish driver Fernando Alonso takes the lead during the 2010 Hungarian Grand Prix.

Leisure

There is a strong coffeehouse culture in Hungary's towns and cities, with people meeting in cafés to chat and socialize. For holidays, people visit mountains and lakes such as Lake Velence and Lake Balaton. Many Hungarians have a summer cottage or hut in the countryside where they relax and grow produce.

There are many festival foods to enjoy at this Christmas market in Budapest.

Food

Traditional Hungarian food tends to be rich and meaty. The national dish is goulash (*gulyás*). This is a soup made with smoked meat and beans. Lots of dishes are made using paprika, a spice made from chilli peppers. Many dishes use sour cream and dumplings. *Kifli* are crescent-shaped bread rolls that have been eaten since the Turks **occupied** Hungary. Desserts include *Dobos* cake, a sponge cake made in five layers with chocolate buttercream and ground nuts.

How to say...

apple *alma* (OL-mo)
cabbage *káposzta* (KAA-paws-to)
cheese *sajt* (SHO-y-t)
chicken *csirke* (CHIR-ke)
egg *tojás* (TAW-yaash)
meat *hús* (hush)
milk *tej* (TE-y)
potato *burgonya* (BOOR-gonya)
sandwich *szendvics* (Sendwitch)
stew *pörkölt* (PEUR-keult)
water *víz* (veez)

Palacsinta

Ask an adult to help you make these delicious pancakes.

Ingredients:

- 3 large eggs, beaten
- 240 ml whole milk
- 80 ml soda water/sparkling water
- 80 ml tap water
- 125 g plain flour
- ½ teaspoon salt
- 2 tablespoons butter

What to do:

1. In a bowl, mix together the eggs, milk, sparkling water, and tap water. Then stir in the flour, sugar, and salt to form a smooth batter.
2. Heat a teaspoon of butter in a small frying pan. Spoon in enough batter to thinly coat the bottom of pan.
3. Cook for 2 minutes on the first side and slightly less time on the second side. The pancake should be lightly browned.
4. Repeat until all the pancakes are made. Then fill with your favourite fillings, such as scrambled eggs, mushrooms, meat or vegetables. Roll or fold into a triangle and serve.

Traditions

Betlehemzes is a Hungarian Christmas tradition when boys and young men visit village houses carrying a model church and a manger. On Easter Monday, boys and men visit female relatives and friends, carrying soda water and perfume. They recite poems to the women before sprinkling them with water and perfume! *Disznotor* is a feast celebrated in winter. People slaughter a pig and then eat it together at a party.

Hungary today

Many older Hungarians have mixed feelings about how the country has changed since the end of **communism**. They can remember days when there was a low crime rate, plenty of jobs, and people looked after each other. The slogan used by the young Pioneers was "together for each other" – but these days most people tend to keep to themselves. There are also worries about the country's **economy**. Some people have reacted to the country's problems by attacking minority groups such as **Jewish** and **Roma** people.

Other Hungarians can see the benefits of living in a **democratic** country. They are now free to travel abroad, and new businesses have been able to flourish. The tourist industry has brought new wealth into the country. If it can survive the economic problems facing the whole world, then the hope is that Hungary will adopt the **euro** as its **currency**.

Hungarian people are very proud of their country. Education, **culture**, and sport are highly valued, and close family ties are very important. But the memories of past suffering are still strong. Hungarians know that a lot of hard work is still needed to ensure a peaceful, secure, and successful future for Hungary.

Why not find out more about this fascinating country and its people?

Daily life

Hungary is the only European country where people give their names with the last name first. For example, the swimmer Krisztina Egerszegi would introduce herself as Egerszegi Krisztina. Titles also use this system, so that Mr Ferenc Liszt would be Liszt Ferenc úr.

These Hungarians are relaxing at a **thermal** spa in Budapest.

Fact file

Official name:	Republic of Hungary
Official language:	Hungarian
Capital city:	Budapest
Bordering countries:	Austria, Croatia, Romania, Serbia, Slovakia, Slovenia, Ukraine
Geographic coordinates:	47 00 N, 20 00 E
Population:	9,880,059
Largest cities (populations):	Budapest (1,712,210) Debrecen (206,225) Miskolc (170,234) Szeged (169,030)
Urban population:	68 per cent of total population
Birth rate:	9.43 births per 1,000 people
Life expectancy (total):	73.69 years
Life expectancy (men):	69.53 years
Life expectancy (women):	78.11 years
Ethnic groups (percentage):	Hungarian (92.3%) **Roma** (1.9%) other or unknown (5.8%)
Religion (percentage):	Roman Catholic (51.9%) Calvinist (15.9%) **Lutheran** (3%) Greek Catholic (2.6%) other **Christian** (1%) other or unspecified (11.1%) no religion (14.5%)
Internet users:	6,176,400 (61.8% of population)
Type of government:	parliamentary **democracy**
National animal:	the Turul, a mythological bird
National symbol:	patriarchal cross † and three mountains
Climate:	cold winters and warm summers

Area (total):	93,028 sq kilometres (35,918 square miles)
land:	89,608 sq kilometres (34,597 square miles)
water:	3,420 sq kilometres (1,320 square miles)
Mountains:	Transdanubian Mountains
	400–700 metres (1,312–2,296 feet)
	Northern Mountains
	500–1000 metres (1,640–3,280 feet)
Major rivers:	Danube – 417 kilometres (259 miles) long in Hungary
	Tisza – 598 kilometres (371.5 miles) long in Hungary
Highest elevation:	Kékes – 1,014 metres (3,326.7 feet) in the Mátra Mountains
Lowest elevation:	Tisza River – 78 metres (255.9 feet)
Currency:	*forint*
Natural resources:	bauxite, coal, natural gas, fertile soils, farming land
Major industries:	mining, metals, construction materials, processed foods, textiles, chemicals, motor vehicles
Main imports:	machinery and equipment, fuels and electricity, food products, raw materials
Main exports:	machinery and equipment, other manufactures, food products, raw materials, fuels, and electricity
Units of measurement:	metric

These folk dancers from the southern Baranya region are wearing traditional Hungarian clothes.

Famous Hungarians

Ferenc Puskás (footballer),
Amerigo Tot (sculptor),
Robert Capa (photographer),
Erno Rubik (inventor of Rubik's Cube),
Lászlo József Bíró (inventor of ballpoint pen),
Oszkár Asbóth (inventor of the helicopter),
Ignaz Philipp Semmelweis (doctor who discovered that hand-washing reduced the spread of infection in hospitals).

These sculptures by Amerigo Tot are in the garden of a museum in Pecs.

National holidays

1 January	New Year's Day
15 March	Revolution of 1848
March/April	Easter
1 May	International Labour Day
May/June	Whit Monday
20 August	St Stephen's Day
23 October	Revolution of 1956
1 November	All Saints Day
25 December	Christmas

Hungarian national anthem

The Hungarian national anthem is very long. The first two verses are:

O Lord, bless the nation of Hungary
With your grace and bounty
Extend over it your guarding arm
During strife with its enemies
Long torn by ill fate
Bring upon it a time of relief
This nation has suffered for all sins
Of the past and of the future!

You brought our ancestors up
Over the Carpathians' holy peaks
By You was won a beautiful homeland
For Bendeguz's sons
And wherever flow the rivers of
The Tisza and the Danube
Árpád our hero's descendants
Will root and bloom.

Timeline

> **BC** is short for "before Christ". BC is added after a date and means that the date occurred before the birth of Jesus Christ, for example, 450 BC.
>
> **AD** is short for *Anno Domini*, which is Latin for "in the year of our Lord". AD is added before a date and means that the date occurred after the birth of Jesus Christ, for example, AD 720.

around 895	The Magyars become powerful in Hungarian lands
around 1000	King Stephen I is crowned king of Hungary
1241	Mongols invade Hungary
1309	Charles I is crowned king of Hungary
1526	Hungarian King Louis II is defeated by the Turks at the Battle of Mohacs. Hungary is separated into three parts with the Turks ruling central Hungary, the Habsburgs ruling west Hungary and Transylvania ruling the east.
1723	Emperor Charles VI allows Hungary to become a separate kingdom in the empire
1844	Magyar replaces German as the official language
1849	The Habsburgs repress a nationalist uprising in Hungary
1867	Austrian Emperor Franz Joseph is crowned king of Hungary and rules Austria-Hungary
1882	Triple **Alliance** is created between Austria-Hungary, Germany and Italy
1914	Austria-Hungary declares war on Serbia. Russia, France, and Britain (the **Allied** powers) declare war on Austria-Hungary. World War I (1914–1918) begins.

1915	Italy declares war on Austria-Hungary
1918	Austria-Hungary surrenders to the Allied powers. The Republic of Hungary is founded.
1920	The Treaty of Trianon divides up central Europe. Hungary loses many lands.
1939	World War II (1939–1945) begins
1941	Hungary is allied to Germany, Italy, and Japan (the Axis powers)
1944–1945	Germany invades Hungary. Hungarian Jews are sent to **concentration camps**, where hundreds of thousands are murdered. Hungary signs an armistice with the **Soviet Union**. The Soviet army enters Hungary and surrounds Budapest.
1945	Germans surrender Budapest, but much of the city is destroyed
1953	Imre Nagy becomes prime minister
1955	Nagy is removed from power
1956	Students protest against hard-line **communism**, and Nagy becomes prime minister again. The uprising is crushed when Soviet troops invade.
1958	Imre Nagy is executed
1989	The electric fence between Hungary and Austria is taken down
1990	Free elections are held. Árpád Göncz is elected president.
1991	The last Soviet troops leave Hungary
1999	Hungary joins **NATO**
2004	Hungary joins the **EU**
2006	Riots take place in Budapest caused by economic problems
2008	The Hungarian government borrows money from the International Monetary Fund (IMF)

Glossary

academic relating to learning or studies

a cappella singing without being accompanied by an instrument

alliance union of two or more sides

Allies countries opposed to Germany, Italy, and Japan in World War II, including the United Kingdom, France, Poland, the Soviet Union, and the United States

Art Nouveau style of art popular in the late 1800s, often using stylised natural forms

Christianity religion based on the teachings of Christ

classical serious, artistic music, often played by an orchestra or piano

communism social system where all people in a country share work and property. People who practise communism are called communists.

concentration camp prison and death camps where people were sent during World War II

culture practices, traditions, and beliefs of a society

currency banknotes and coins accepted in exchange for goods and services

democracy system of government where the people of a country elect representatives to a parliament

economy to do with the money, industry, and jobs in a country

embroidery textiles that are sewn with decorative stitches

emissions amount of pollution caused by burning of fuels

endangered in danger of extinction

euro type of currency used in many European countries

EU (European Union) organization of European countries with shared political and economic aims

export transport and sell goods to another country

Expressionist style of painting that exaggerates lines and colours to have a powerful affect

geological natural features, composition, and history of the land in a particular region

ghetto area in a city where a minority group lives separately

head of state main public representative of a country, such as a queen or president

import bring in a product, resource, or service from another country

industrialized when industry is introduced on a large scale

infrastructure networks and structures needed for a society to function, such as roads, power supplies, communications, and buildings

Jewish person of the Jewish religion, ethnicity, or culture. Jewish people trace their roots back to the ancient Hebrew people of Israel.

landlocked country with no coast

liberal in favour of progress and individual freedom

Lutheran follower of Christianity with beliefs that are different to those of Catholics

NATO (North Atlantic Treaty Organization) organization that includes the United States, Canada, and many European countries in which members give each other military help

Nazi member of the National Socialist Party in Germany in the 1930s and 1940s

nomadic relating to people who move from place to place

occupy when people from one region or country take over another by force

prefabricated building made of factory-made parts that can be quickly put together

reform improve by making changes

renewable energy source of energy that will not run out, such as sunlight, or that can be regrown, such as wood

Roma minority group in Europe, also known as gypsies

rural in the countryside

Soviet Union communist state made up of Russia and its former empire, in existence between 1922 and 1991

thermal relating to heat or temperature

tribe independent social group, historically often made up of nomadic peoples

vocational related to a profession or occupation

West refers to a group of developed nations with similar political systems and values, including the United States, the European Union, Canada, Australia, and New Zealand

Find out more

Books

Easy Menu Ethnic Cookbooks: Cooking the Hungarian Way, Magdolna Hargittai (Lerner Publishing Group, 2007)

Lonely Planet Guide to Hungary, Neal Bedford (Lonely Planet, 2009)

National Geographic Kids World Atlas (National Geographic Society, 2010)

The Usborne Encyclopedia of World History, Jane Bingham, Fiona Chandler, and Sam Taplin (Usborne, 2009)

Websites

www.hungary.org.uk/hungarian-cultural-centre.asp
This website from the Hungarian Cultural Centre in London has lots of information about Hungarian culture. It will also help you find out more about Hungarian people in the United Kingdom.

http://hungary.embassyhomepage.com
Visit the website of the Hungarian Embassy in London to see maps of Hungary. You can also find out information about the weather, holidays, money, and the Hungarian language.

www.budapestinfo.hu/en
You can get a good idea about life in Budapest by visiting the city's official tourist website.

http://www.cia.gov/library/publications/the-world-factbook/geos/hu/html
The CIA World Factbook is full of fascinating information about Hungary.

Places to visit

If you ever get the chance to go to Hungary, here are just some of the many places you could visit:

Budapest parks

In Budapest, you might enjoy visiting Városligeti Park which contains an amusement park, a circus, and a zoo. Margaret Island on the River Danube is also a great place to relax.

The Hungarian Railway Museum

The Hungarian Railway Museum is full of old steam trains, and there are lots of activities for you to take part in.

Budapest Castle District

Visit the Castle District in Budapest to see its amazing little streets and buildings, as well as a fantastic view of the city.

Lake Balaton

You can enjoy swimming, sailing, boat trips, birdwatching, horse riding, bike rides, and exploring caves on Lake Balaton's many beaches.

Debrecen

The city of Debrecen is on Hungary's Great Plain, where you can see cowboys demonstrating their horsemanship.

Aggtelek

Visit the village of Aggtelek in the northern uplands of Hungary to see an amazing network of caves, full of incredible stalactites, stalagmites, and huge chambers.

Topic tools

You can use these topic tools for your school projects. Trace the map on to a sheet of paper, using the thick black outlines to guide you.

The Hungarian flag was inspired by the French flag during the Hungarian Revolution of 1848. The colours used come from the country's historical coat of arms. Copy the flag design and then colour in your picture. Make sure you use the right colours!

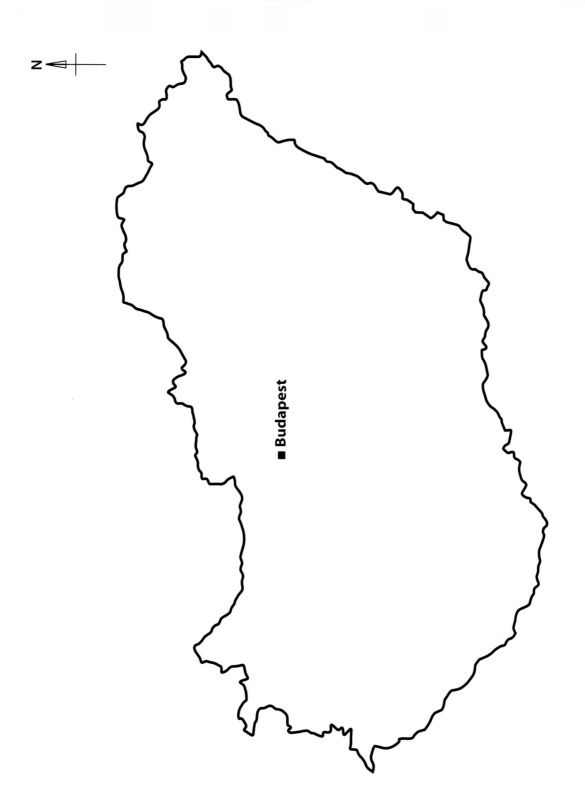

N

■ Budapest

Index